FAST TRACK

Wrestle Mania

Main Features

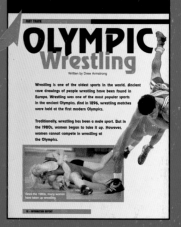

Other Features

SUMO Wrestling

Written by Nicholas Cheng

The sport of wrestling takes many forms. But perhaps one of the most interesting is sumo wrestling. Sumo wrestling is a contest between two very large wrestlers. The object of a sumo match is for one wrestler to knock the other wrestler down or out of a ring. Wrestlers push, pull, tug, slap, and dodge each other. They do these things in order to cause their opponent to fall or go outside the ring.

According to Japanese legend, a Japanese god entered a sumo match with a god from an enemy tribe. The Japanese god won the match. This win proved the dominance of the Japanese people. From then on, they ruled the islands that are now known as Japan.

Sumo wrestling began more than 2,000 years ago. The first sumo matches were connected to religion. The matches were the Japanese people's way of thanking the gods for a good harvest. This meant that the matches would always include prayers and sacred dances. When sumo first started so long ago, wrestlers would do almost anything to win. Sometimes, they would even kill their opponents. Over the years, sumo slowly changed into the sport it is today.

▶▶▶

Sumo Wrestlers

Sumo wrestlers are called **rikishi**. Each wrestler chooses a poetic name for himself. There is one thing that is quite noticeable about the rikishi – they are very big. Their weight can range from 280–450 pounds (135–230 kg).

Rikishi work hard to make their stomachs big. Their big stomachs help give them a low center of gravity. This makes it harder to knock a rikishi out of the ring.

To get this big, the rikishi eat large amounts of high-protein food. In particular, there is a special stew called **chanko-nabe**. This special stew is made of bite-sized chunks of beef, chicken, pork, fish, tofu, vegetables, soy sauce, and other things.

When they are wrestling, rikishi wear nothing on their feet. They are naked except for a loincloth, called a **mawashi**. A mawashi is made from colorful silk cloth or black cotton. It is about 30 feet (9 m) long and it is wrapped several times around a wrestler's waist and between his legs. Wrestlers are allowed to grab an opponent's mawashi during a match in order to throw him out of the ring.

Rikishi grow their hair long. During matches, they wear their hair in a knot. The style of the knot differs according to the wrestler's rank. The lower the rank, the plainer the knot. The knot helps protect the wrestler's head if he falls.

> To get this big, the rikishi eat large amounts of high-protein food.

Learning Sumo

Japanese rikishi learn the sport of sumo at one of more than 25 schools in Japan. Young wrestlers usually enter the school by the age of 15. After that, they go through years of training. Rikishi compete in many matches each year. Since there are no weight classes in sumo, the lighter wrestlers have to rely on quickness and skill to defeat larger wrestlers.

The lighter wrestler will need to use speed and skill to defeat his heavier opponent.

The Rules of Sumo

Sumo wrestlers have many moves in a match. These moves consist of throws, twists, lifts, shoves, grabs, and slaps. They are not allowed to hit their opponent with a closed fist. They cannot pull hair, claw at the eyes, or choke their opponent. And they are not allowed to kick an opponent in the stomach.

Sumo matches are won when a rikishi forces his opponent out of the ring or throws him to the ground. A match is lost if any part of the wrestler's body, other than his feet, touches the ground inside the ring.

The wrestler on the ground has lost this sumo match.

Sumo Matches

Sumo matches take place in a ring called a **dohyo**. The dohyo is 18 square feet (1.7 sq m) and raised 2 feet (0.6 m) off the ground. It is made of a special type of clay. The hard clay is covered with a thin layer of sand. A circle 15 feet (4.6 m) in diameter is drawn in the middle of the dohyo. The contest takes place inside this circle. A roof is suspended over the dohyo. It makes the dohyo look like a shrine.

A sumo tournament consists of several matches. Before the tournament begins there is an entry ceremony. Each team of wrestlers walks down the aisle to the ring. The last person to enter the ring is the grand champion. He claps his hands to get the attention of the gods and raises and stomps down each foot to chase evil from the ring.

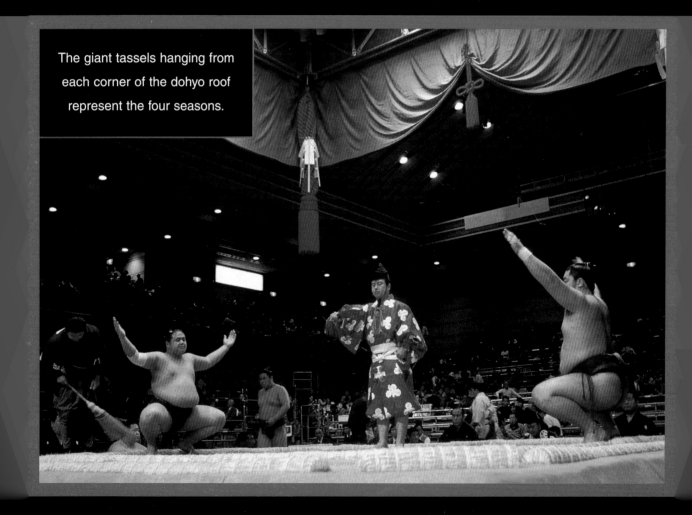

The giant tassels hanging from each corner of the dohyo roof represent the four seasons.

He claps his hands to get the attention of the gods and raises and stomps down each foot to chase evil from the ring.

Rikishi perform many traditional moves before a sumo tournament.

Before a match begins, the rikishi go through another ritual. The ritual includes rinsing their mouths with water and wiping their bodies with paper towels. They raise one leg high to the side of their body. Then they bring their foot down, stomping it hard on the ground. They repeat this same movement with the other leg. While doing this, they raise their arms to their sides. Finally, each wrestler grabs a handful of salt. They rub salt on their bodies and scatter it around the ring. The salt is to purify the ring and their bodies.

A low-ranking assistant called a yobidashi announces the names of the rikishi in a high-pitched voice. The wrestlers then squat and face each other. They look fiercely at one another, each of them trying to unsettle his opponent. A wrestling match lasts between one or two minutes. After the last match, there is a short closing ritual to signal that the tournament has finished.

SUMO
WRESTLING

Coming in March
Two Giants of Sumo

Who will win?

SUMO
Shopping List

For one week's supply of chanko-nabe

5 chickens

10 onions

20 carrots

15 negi (green onions)

5 daikon (long white radishes)

5 large potatoes

50 shiitake mushrooms

5 cabbages

10 cakes of aburage (deep-fried tofu)

10 cakes of fresh tofu

1 large bottle of soy sauce

1 sack of rice

Sumo DETECTIVE

Written by Emma Slater
Illustrated by Graham Tavendale

"That was one great movie!" Joel said. "The fight scene with the bad guys at the end was wicked, man."

"What about that detective who took on six guys and beat them all?" said Darin. "What a guy!"

"And what about the car chase?" said Henry. "The way that tanker blew up – it was so real. Was it a real tanker or a model?"

"It looked real, but who can tel[l] these days?" said Darin. "They car[n] do some wicked stuff with specia[l] effects. That would be a cool job[.] Maybe I'll do special effects when [I] leave school."

"I want to be a detective and bea[t] up all the bad dudes," said Joel.

"You?" laughed Henry. "You're too[o] small to beat up anybody. Darin's the[e] sumo wrestler. He should be a[a] detective – he'd easily beat up all the[e] bad dudes."

"How's your sumo wrestling going?" Joel asked Darin. "Can you show us some of your moves?"

"Are you kidding?" laughed Henry again. "You couldn't even begin to do sumo wrestling. Darin would kill you."

"You're not the biggest guy around yourself," replied Joel angrily. "Just because I'm not big, that doesn't mean I can't be a sumo wrestler, does it, Darin?"

"Actually," said Darin, "you do have to be a certain height and weight to be a sumo wrestler. Henry's right, you're just not big enough."

Joel kicked a can that was lying on the street in front of him.

"It's just not fair,"

he moaned. "I eat like a horse and I just don't get any bigger. I guess it's because my dad's small. I'm never going to be big enough to be a sumo wrestler."

"Hey, not everyone can be a sumo wrestler, you know," said Darin. "But you can come to my studio and watch me train any time you like."

"OK," said Joel, perking up.

"But I don't really think you're cut out for such an early morning start, are you?"

asked Darin. "Or the kitchen duty, or the cleaning, or..."

"OK, OK, enough," said Joel. "You're right. I'm not an early riser, but I'm definitely coming to watch you tomorrow."

"No problem, little buddy," said Darin. "I'll see you at four o'clock tomorrow morning."

Joel's jaw dropped.

"Well, maybe not tomorrow," he mumbled.

"Hi, guys," said a voice from behind them. 'Nice night for a walk."

Joel, Darin, and Henry stopped laughing and looked around. They had been so busy talking, they hadn't noticed that they had walked into the Bays Boys' territory. Joel, Darin, and Henry's usual routine was to walk the long way home from the movies to avoid the pier, which was where the Bays Boys hung out.

The Bays Boys were bullies who were a couple of years older than them. They always wore black – black shoes, black jeans, and black T-shirts. They picked on the smaller kids at school and punched them when the teachers weren't around.

The voice the three friends had heard was the Bays Boys' leader Jack – and he was not alone.

Henry and Joel looked at each other nervously. They were surrounded.

"Go on, Darin," whispered Joel, "you can take them out. Do sumo moves on them."

"What was that, pinhead?" sneered Jack. "In case you hadn't noticed, pipsqueak, there're six of us, and only three of you. Even big boy here can't get you out of this one."

Joel gulped fearfully as he heard laughter come from the other boys in the gang. "We're history!" he moaned.

"Seeing I'm such a nice guy," said Jack, "I'm going to give you two minutes to think about what we should do with you. Then, you're history!"

The three friends huddled together. While Joel and Henry had been more worried about what was going on, Darin had been looking around to see what they could do. He realized they were on the part of the pier where the fishermen brought in their catches. There were nets and ropes everywhere.

"Listen up," Darin whispered to Joel and Henry. "I'm not going to fight these jerks."

"Why not?" whispered Joel. "You're a sumo wrestler, you could easily beat them."

"It's just not right to fight when you don't need to," replied Darin.

"What do you mean, you don't need to fight?"

asked Henry. "If you don't fight, we're all going to get beaten up!"

"I've got a plan," whispered Darin. "See that rope just to your left, Henry?"

Henry nodded.

"When I say *go*, pull it hard," said Darin. "It's connected to the fishing nets up there. The nets will fall down and trap the three dudes on the left. Don't look up now, just trust me."

"OK," whispered Henry, "but what about the other three?"

"Joel's going to take care of them," replied Darin.

"Me?" gulped Joel.

"Sure," replied Darin. "See that rope by your feet? It's tied to the pier. When they make their move, pull the rope hard. It'll trip up the three dudes on the right. I'll grab the end and wind it round them. That'll keep them quiet for a while."

"Stop whispering!" yelled Jack.

"Come and make us!" shouted back Darin.

"What are you doing?" hissed Joel.

"They need to be closer for the plan to work," Darin whispered.

"Let's get 'em!" screamed Jack.

"Go!" shouted Darin at the same time.

Henry reached over and pulled hard on the rope. The net dropped on three of the Bays Boys, trapping them underneath. There were shouts as the boys thrashed around, trying to get free.

Then Joel pulled hard on the other rope and tripped up the other three. They were taken by surprise. Quick as a flash, Darin grabbed the rope and ran around the boys and tied them up tight.

"Run for it, before they get loose!" Darin shouted.

They ran down the pier as fast as they could and only stopped after they put a couple of blocks between themselves and the pier.

"That was great!" said Henry with a smile, sucking in his breath. "We beat the Bays Boys!"

"That's right," said Darin. "And we didn't even lay a hand on them."

"How did you think up all that stuff?" asked Joel. "I wouldn't have even been able to begin to think up a plan like that."

"Sure you would," replied Darin. "It's only a matter of doing a little detective work. Joel, you want to be a detective, don't you? So you just need to look around you and see what can help you."

"Yeah," said Henry. "It looks like you were right, Darin. Fighting isn't always the answer."

"That's right,"

said Darin. "If we'd fought them, we'd have been hurt for sure. No matter how good we were, there were six of them, remember. Anyway, brains will always beat brawn. All we have to do now is figure out what to do at school on Monday."

Olympic Wrestling Divisions

Olympic wrestling competitions take place between teams from many countries. Each team has wrestlers in different weight classes. There are eight different weight classes for wrestlers to compete in.

Weight Class	Weight
Flyweight	115 pounds (52 kg)
Bantamweight	125 pounds (57 kg)
Featherweight	137 pounds (62 kg)
Lightweight	150 pounds (68 kg)
Welterweight	163 pounds (74 kg)
Middleweight	180 pounds (82 kg)
Light Heavyweight	198 pounds (90 kg)
Super Heavyweight	287 pounds (130 kg)

Olympic Wrestling Arena

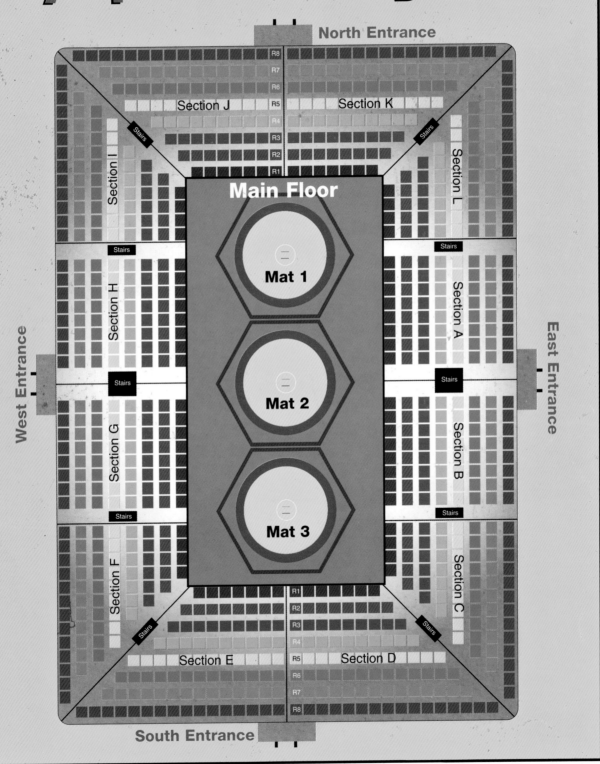

North Entrance

Section J   R8 R7 R6 R5 R4 R3 R2 R1   Section K

Stairs   Stairs

Section I   Section L

Main Floor

Mat 1

West Entrance   **East Entrance**

Stairs   Section H   Section A   Stairs

Stairs   Stairs

Section G   Mat 2   Section B

Stairs   Stairs

Section F   Mat 3   Section C

Stairs   Stairs

Section E   R1 R2 R3 R4 R5 R6 R7 R8   Section D

South Entrance

OLYMPIC Wrestling

Written by Drew Armstrong

Wrestling is one of the oldest sports in the world. Ancient cave drawings of people wrestling have been found in Europe. Wrestling was one of the most popular sports in the ancient Olympics. And in 1896, wrestling matches were held at the first modern Olympics.

Traditionally, wrestling has been a male sport. But in the 1980s, women began to take it up. However, women cannot compete in wrestling at the Olympics.

Since the 1980s, many women have taken up wrestling.

Amateur Wrestling

Amateur wrestling is very different from the professional wrestling seen on television. It is a serious sport. It takes a lot of training. Amateur wrestlers do not wrestle for money, they wrestle for the love of the sport.

The top goal of nearly every amateur wrestler is to compete at the Olympics. A successful wrestler needs endurance, strength, intelligence, and the will to train hard.

A successful wrestler needs endurance, strength, intelligence, and the will to train hard.

Wrestling Equipment

Wrestling does not require much equipment. Wrestlers wear a tight-fitting, one-piece suit called a **singlet**. They can also wear headgear to protect their ears and to keep their hair hidden. Light, soft-soled shoes are worn on the feet. Thin kneepads can also be worn. The match takes place on a mat made of special material that cushions wrestlers. The wrestling area is a circle, 9 feet (2.8 m) in diameter.

Amateur wrestlers do not wear fancy costumes.

Types of Olympic Wrestling

There are two different types of Olympic wrestling – freestyle and Greco-Roman. In many ways, they are similar. In both types of wrestling, a match is won when one wrestler presses their opponent's shoulders against the wrestling mat. This is called a fall or **pin**.

There are small ways in which the two types of wrestling are different.

Freestyle is the most popular type of wrestling. Freestyle wrestlers can use all parts of their body. But in Greco-Roman wrestling, all of the holds must be above the waist. Greco-Roman wrestlers are not allowed to use their legs to hold or take down an opponent.

A wrestler is not beaten until both shoulders have been pressed to the mat.

In both types of wrestling, a match is won when one wrestler presses their opponent's shoulders against the wrestling mat.

Olympic Wrestling Matches

Olympic wrestling matches are split into two time periods, each lasting three minutes. The match ends if one wrestler is able to score a fall or pin, or score a 10-point advantage over their opponent. If neither wrestler scores a fall or pin, the wrestler who scores the most points wins. If neither wrestler has more than three points, or, if they have the same number of points, there is an overtime period. Overtime lasts no more than three minutes. If the match is still tied after the overtime, the referee names the winner.

Olympic wrestling matches have a referee, a judge, and a chairman, who give points to the wrestlers and make sure they follow the rules. For points to be awarded, two of the three officials have to agree that the point has been scored.

▶▶▶

Scoring Points

Fall or Pin

A fall or pin is when a wrestler manages to pin their opponent's shoulders to the mat for one second. No points are given for a fall or pin because it is an automatic win for the wrestler who does the move successfully.

Near Fall

If a wrestler is able to turn their opponent's back toward the mat, but not press the opponent's back against the mat, they can score points. They almost pin the opponent and that is why it is called a near fall. Near falls score the most points.

Takedown

A wrestler can score points by a **takedown**. A takedown happens when one wrestler forces their opponent to the mat from a standing position. If a wrestler takes down an opponent onto their back, extra points are scored.

Reversal

If a wrestler who is being controlled by an opponent is able to reverse positions and take control, they will be awarded points for the **reversal**.

Escape

A wrestler who is being controlled by an opponent but is able to escape and get to their feet wins points.

Getting to the Olympics

It is a long, hard road to get to wrestle at the Olympics, but the rewards are great for the few wrestlers who make it. Competitors will be wrestling with the best in the world. And, they also get the chance to bring home an Olympic medal.

TAG!

Written by Josephine Selwyn

Tag, sumo, or just plain mud,
Wrestling fever's in my blood.

I take it in every match I can,
I must be wrestling's biggest fan.

I watch those tag guys in the ring,
Last night I saw a tag team fling.

One guy was called the Prince of Hope,
He bounced Big Dave right off the rope.

They faked the blow and hit the deck,
They were really going neck to neck.

Then Big Dave tagged the Mean Machine,
He was the biggest guy I ever had seen!

He chased the Prince and made him dance,
Poor old Prince never had a chance.

The match ended with the Prince on his back,
The Mean Machine was on the attack!

JADE Gets Even

Written by Chris Paul
Illustrated by Kelvin Hawley

"Josh, you know the rules," said Coach Wright. "There will be no girls' wrestling team while I'm the wrestling coach."

"But Jade and her friends are really good, Coach," said Josh.

"Look, Josh, I'm not going to change my mind about this," replied Coach Wright. "Most boys are stronger than girls. I don't want girls getting hurt in a match and then coming crying to me. Anyway, we've only had boys' wrestling teams at this school and it's not going to change while I'm here. And that's the end of it!"

Jade was hiding under the main stand, listening to Josh trying to change Coach Wright's mind. She couldn't believe her ears.

"Cry during a match!" thought Jade. "I don't think so!"

Where had this jerk been for the last hundred years? Did he still think girls passed out when they saw blood? Jade was angry.

"I'll show you," she said to herself.

Later that afternoon, she found Josh. She was still annoyed with Coach Wright.

"I heard what he told you," she said.

"I'm sorry, Jade," Josh said. "I really tried. But Coach has got this thing about girls and wrestling."

"Why don't the other coaches say something to him?" Jade asked. "What would happen if they didn't let girls swim or play tennis? It's just so frustrating."

"I know," Josh said. "Yesterday, I told him that there are more girls than boys playing soccer. But he just won't listen."

"I guess I'll just have to find something else to do," said Jade. "Thanks, anyway. I'll see you at home."

When Jade got home she was still angry. She was a better wrestler than half the boys on the wrestling team. She'd been wrestling with Josh ever since he took it up. Now she was as good as he was. She knew other girls who would be good wrestlers, too. She'd gone to Coach Wright, and that's when she found out the *No Girls* rule. She'd tried everything she could think of to get him to have a girls' team, but the answer was always the same.

"I'LL get even with the coach somehow,"

Jade said to herself. "I've just got to think of how to do it so I can prove him wrong!"

Jade's older sister, Jessica, came in the door.

"Hi, Jade," she said. "How did Josh get on with Coach Wright today?"

"No good," replied Jade. "He won't change. He's just too hardheaded."

"Why don't you take up judo like me?" asked Jessica. "It's almost the same as wrestling. I think you'd be really good at judo. It takes just as much skill as wrestling."

"I guess I could give it a try while I'm thinking of a way to prove my point to Coach Wright," said Jade.

"What have I got to lose?"

So the next day, Jade joined the local judo club. Her mother bought her a uniform and Jessica took her down to the dojo and introduced her to the sensei.

"Hi, Jade," the sensei said. "Why don't you join the rest of the class on the mat? We're just about ready to begin."

The first hour went by quickly. At the end of the session, Jade was hot and sweaty but she'd had a great time.

"It was awesome!" she told Josh when she got home. "I'm going to love judo."

"You didn't hurt yourself when you were thrown to the mat?" asked her mother.

"Not a bit," Jade replied. "Learning how to fall is all part of judo. That's why it's so good. You learn how to fall so you don't hurt yourself."

"Better judo than wrestling then," said Josh. "Coach Wright doesn't teach us how to fall properly. The boys on the team are always getting hurt."

"Really?" said Jade, an idea forming in her mind.

"You never told me that before."

▶▶▶

The days and weeks went by fast. Jade went to judo twice a week. She still wrestled with Josh when she had some free time. She had to learn judo quickly if she was going to put her plan into action. At the end of eight weeks, she talked to the sensei about her idea.

"Anything that cuts down on sports injuries is good, Jade," he said. "I'll help you as much as I can."

That night, Jade told Josh her plan.

"You know how you said the boys on the wrestling team are always getting injured," she began.

"Yeah," replied Josh. "It's no big deal though, everyone gets injured."

"Well, what would you say if I told you I could teach the guys on the team how to fall so they don't get hurt?" said Jade.

"I'd say, dream on," replied Josh.

"Listen, then," said Jade. "The first thing you learn in judo is how to fall so you don't hurt yourself. I could teach you. Just try it before you say no. If you still think it's stupid after your next match, I'll stop bugging you."

"OK then," said Josh.

▶▶▶

Jade and Josh worked together for the next hour. By the end of the hour, Josh was impressed. He called up the rest of the team and soon Jade was teaching her first class.

The boys on the wrestling team worked with Jade every day after school. The sensei came the first three times to make sure Jade was teaching them correctly. The boys got better and better at taking the falls without getting hurt. Their wrestling improved, too.

After a month, Coach Wright noticed something different about his team. But he couldn't figure out what it was.

"How come you boys are winning matches without getting hurt?" he asked. "We've always had one or two of you out with an injury before."

"We can show you after school tomorrow, if you like," replied Seth, the team captain.

"OK," said Coach Wright. "I'll see you in the gym after school."

So the next day, Coach Wright walked into the gym after school.

"What's this?" shouted Coach Wright when he saw Jade. "I thought I told you, no girls' wrestling team."

"Hold it, Coach," said Seth. "It's not how it looks."

"So tell me what it is then," said Coach Wright angrily.

"Jade's been teaching us how to fall without hurting ourselves," said Seth. "She's been going to judo since you wouldn't allow the girls to have a wrestling team. She learned how to fall without hurting herself and now she's teaching us."

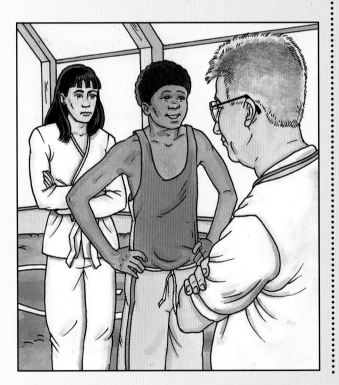

"So you think you're the coach now, do you?" said Coach Wright, turning to Jade. "Think you know it all, do you?"

"No," replied Jade. "I don't think I'm the coach, and I don't think I know it all. What I do know, though, is that girls can do things that boys can do. Girls can play body contact sports without getting hurt and crying."

"Is that so?" asked Coach Wright. "You think I'll let you and your friends have a wrestling team now, do you? Well, you're wrong. There'll be no girls' wrestling team while I'm the coach. So nothing's changed."

"Everything's changed," replied Jade. "You see, I don't want to have a girls' wrestling team anymore. I'm enjoying judo. I'm good at it, and I'm going to get my black belt one day. I started out wanting to prove you wrong about girls and wrestling. But I don't anymore. All I want is to have a coach who respects what girls can do. And I want to help these guys so they don't get hurt."

Coach Wright turned and left the gym without another word.

"Don't worry, Jade," Seth said. "He'll come around one day. It just takes some people longer than others to change their views on some things."

Judo/Wrestling Comparison Chart

Judo	Freestyle Wrestling
Two participants	Two participants
Points scoring system	Points scoring system
Different weight divisions	Different weight divisions
Bare feet	Soft-soled shoes are worn
Three officials (a referee and two corner judges)	Three officials (a referee, a judge, and a chairman)
Minimum of two of the three referees must agree when points are awarded	Minimum of two of the three officials must agree when points are awarded
No headgear	Headgear
Belts to signify rank	No belts
A match lasts up to five minutes	Match lasts five minutes with three minutes overtime if the match is tied at full-time *Note: Olympic wrestling matches have two three-minute periods
Competition area is 26 feet (8 m) long by 26 feet (8 m) wide	Competition area has a diameter of 9 feet (2.8 m)
Each move is given marks according to how well it is performed	Each move is worth a certain number of points

GLOSSARY for *Sumo Wrestling*

chanko-nabe – A type of high-protein stew that is traditionally eaten by rikishi.

The rikishi was eating his ninth bowl of **chanko-nabe**.

dohyo – A sumo wrestling ring. A sumo wrestling match always happens within a circle.

The circle is part of the **dohyo**, or raised platform, where sumo wrestling takes place.

mawashi – The loincloth worn by all rikishi.

When wrestling, a rikishi wears only a **mawashi**.

rikishi – A sumo wrestler.

Although he was very large, the **rikishi** moved gracefully around the room.

GLOSSARY for *Olympic Wrestling*

pin – A wrestling move where one wrestler presses another wrestler's shoulders against the wrestling mat.

Johnny had won the wrestling match when he had Tony in a **pin**.

reversal – One wrestler gains control over his or her opponent by reversing their positions on the mat.

In a close finish, June used a **reversal** move to turn the match to her advantage.

singlet – A tight-fitting one-piece suit worn by wrestlers.

When taking part in a wrestling match, a wrestler must wear a **singlet**.

takedown – Forcing an opponent to the mat from a standing position.

In order to get extra points, Glen forced Sam to the mat in a **takedown**.